When Pain Speaks, *Faith Answers*

A transformative collection of heartfelt poems, short stories, and devotions illuminating God's restorative work in broken vessels.

ANTOINETTE VERNICE
IRIZARRY-GRAVES

When Pain Speaks, Faith Answers

ISBN: 979-8-218-78413-3

Publishing in the United States of America

Publisher: Utterance Media LLC,

utterancemediallc@gmail.com

Cover Illustration: Karolyne Roberts, Luminous Publishing

Interior Design: Muhtashin Fuad

Cover Photography: The Lx Studios

Table of Contents

PART III

THE PLAN

Dedication

To Allan, Jr, and Ava, I'm grateful you didn't receive a broken me. May you hold fast to your faith in Jesus Christ, no matter what happens! With Jesus, you can do anything!

To my younger self, you are loved, forgiven, and transformed. You have returned to that bold, immovable girl with the help of many people. You are living your best life with Jesus Christ!

Author's Cogitation

This book should not be placed in your hands.

I attempted several times to end this assignment, but midwives, Karolyne Roberts of Luminous Publishing, and Victoria Johnson of By Victoria, LLC, would not let me. I thank them with my entire soul for allowing me to think long, wide, deep, and within increments. They carefully held and nurtured my story in the palm of their hands to help me birth this initial print. Because of them and the help of the Holy Spirit, a portion of my life is finally placed in your hands.

Cherish it as I have.

An Introduction to Faith and Pain

People often ask- How did you develop that perspective? - an introspective lens to see and honor viewpoints, and a thought process to think deeply and intimately, but still reach others?

It's difficult to answer that question. How do I explain my mind? So, I thought back to when I lost my mind and what developed from *that* thought process: *Faith and Pain.*

Pain, trauma, regret, sin, and condemnation can *fracture* our beliefs in Jesus Christ. Once we accept Jesus Christ as our Lord and Savior, our salvation becomes the foundation, but then life's issues, twists and turns, and unexpected and planned circumstances can become *bricks* to harden or *bones* to strengthen our connection with Jesus Christ.

As I maneuvered through pain and trauma in my teens and early 20s, I had to dig deep into my beliefs about Jesus and ask myself if I was aligning with those beliefs in my everyday walk.

I told myself often:
"I'm blessed! I'm not hurt."
"The Lord fights my battles."
"I'm healed in Jesus' Name"

While those statements are true, I still felt broken, stuck, and empty on the inside.

My body felt trapped – to either keep the faith or my pain. I heard throughout my life to *"praise the Lord at all times"* and *"praise your way through,"* but my body wanted to release. A tug-of-war was raging to remain "presentable" in certain spaces rather than giving my body and heart permission to be transparent, raw, and authentic. So, I concealed my heart from God.

Eventually, my faith and pain could not coexist without proper guidance. The Lord met me at my complexities and whispered, *"I am with you. I understand."* I let go of my fear of being disowned as His daughter, surrendered my preconceived notions about bringing my pain to the Lord, and decided to walk with Him. I learned that God does not want us to choose between our faith and our pain. But rather, He desires to use *both* to transform us into His likeness.

Once we trust the Lord with our pain, we can lean on our faith that God will restore us. With the Holy Spirit's help, God empowers His children to fully embody His holiness, wholeness, and convictions here on Earth as it is in Heaven.

We can be renewed, equipped, and restored with the help of Jesus and our community. Because of Him, we can stand firm again.

We are not called to carry faith and pain alone.

Will you answer the call to be transformed?

How To Use This Book

As you read my heartfelt poems, short stories, and devotions, meditate on these questions if they resonate with you:

1) Have I used resources on Earth - shopping, makeup, traveling - to cover up pain?
2) Am I too prideful to admit that I'm hurting on the inside?
3) Do I trust Jesus with my pain?
4) Am I running from accountability and avoiding certain conversations?
5) Am I offended by God?
6) Can I accept correction from people?
7) Am I hiding the truth from the Lord?
8) Do I know how to meditate on Holy Scriptures during painful encounters?

My story paints a transformative journey of restorative power from brokenness to wholeness. It begins with sexual, emotional, and medical **pain** that questioned my identity in Jesus Christ. How the Lord **placed** me in different environments to learn about Him and myself. Then, He designed specific **plans** to restore me physically, spiritually, and mentally so I can stand firm again. It ends with **planting** heartfelt devotions of His Holy Scriptures in our hearts to remind us that faith has answers to our pain. Sounds familiar? The Lord had a redemptive and restorative plan since the Garden of Eden to save His people from darkness and sin after 42 generations. The Lord has plans to restore you, too!

Take your time as you read each section of my story. I pray my story in how the Lord restored me colors a picture of His faithful presence, persistent pursuit, mercy, forgiveness, holiness, and unfailing love.

How wonderful is our Lord!

PART I

The Pain

--Important Notice--

Some circumstances may cause difficult emotions.
Proceed with caution.

Seduced

August 2007

10 frames

1 bowling game

I didn't know I was the goal

Between colognes and work clothes

I could smell their brands

Bodies so close

A wave wasn't enough

"Just take the hug!

Don't scream! Don't make a scene!"

~~My choice~~...gone

Strike!

Frame #1 down

"What's your name?"

"Toni Hollywud"

My hair, my smile, my eyes received many compliments

But it didn't phase me

5 pins down

When I turned away, I felt their eyes staring back, wanting more

They thought, "Persistence"

Missed spare!

"How can I get her attention?"

Frame #2 down

"Can we leave?" "Can we talk?"

My "No's" fueled their desire

6 pins down

They needed a spare this time

They got help

Befriended close relatives

Learned my preferences

Quoted my schedule

Persuasive talks turned soft ears

Trust was built

My number was given

But not by me

They got the *spare*

~~My privacy~~...gone

Frame #3 down

Their eyes of desire
Watched carefully to score on me
Got nothing to lose
Played pots all night
What's one more gamble with a *teen*?
14 years *young*
Their patience endured
Posture strong
Discretion perfected
Confidence clothed them.

They *studied me*
Found an opening
Got my attention
Talked my language
No longer did I want Friday night movies
Skating
Hot Cheetos with cheese and meat
At the corner store
My appetite changed to see them every day
~~My teen innocence~~...gone

Strike!
Strike!
Strike!

Frames #4, #5, #6 down

I missed them
"Where did they go?"
Disappointment when we didn't meet at the alley
at tournaments
at practices
"Where are you?!!"
I rearranged sports and church activities, and you
aren't here!
Text me back! Don't leave me on read
What I once loved, now I want you
How did I get this deep?
How did I lose my way?
Distracted
Strike!
~~My goals~~...gone

Frame #7 down

I stepped into custom shoes

Playing in their world

What's the rules?

What's the cost?

My silence?

You got it

~~My will~~...gone

Frame #8

Strike!

Frame #9

Strike!

~~My determination~~...gone

~~My time~~...gone

It's theirs now

A strong hold like a brace

Like thump tape

Wrapped around their fingers

And then

They touched me

~~My body~~...gone

Frame #10

Strike!

Strike!

Strike!

GAME OVER

Separated

January 2009

Sin

To separate the set apart
from the Divine's appointed plans.
It can't separate Divinity from humanity,
so separate humanity from Divinity instead.

Separated

Designed to be anointed, but now appointed
for men's desires.
I once felt the presence of the Lord walking with me,
but now the warmth of His rage with Adam and Eve
follows me.

Detached

I ran into their arms
instead of the arms of the One who created me
so beautifully and wonderfully made, but my soul
didn't know it.

I was once awestruck by the One, but now I desire more.
The One just wasn't enough.

Dissatisfied
Auditioning to be like Gomer, prostituting my body to the men with the highest time to satisfy my appetite:
(Disregard the One who created time)
"Can you see me?" Validate me!
"Can you hear me?" Affirm me!
(Wait, Antoinette! That's Jehovah El-Roi! Remember Him? Seek Him!)
Naw, the One still isn't enough

I needed physical touch.
Sharing stories and sweat.
Call it "wise beyond years," but really
"groomed to be an adult"
At 15, growing up too fast.

Unprotected
While lying on my back
watching, the pad catching innocent blood being shed.
16 years *young*

Guilt ate from within and wore better than designer clothes.

I couldn't tell. I *shouldn't* tell.

Statutory rape belongs behind bars.

But they can't go away! Even though I was living behind theirs.

Silenced

It was easier to chew than confess.

I know the Lord said to bring all confessions to receive forgiveness, but did *my* sins make it to the Cross?

The old, rugged Cross

That turned a tree branch into a barrier that separated the Son from the Father.

Jesus held onto the cross, carried it for miles, with the help of Simon, to save *me.*

"But No, Jesus! I'll carry my sins myself! I can't give it up! I must see the end."

Death

Death to living a full life

Death to my goals

Death to my body

Death to my innocence

Death to my autonomy
Death to the appetite for holiness
Death to the satisfaction of Jesus
Death to my daily talks with Jesus
Death to recognizing me
That's the meaning of sin

Separation

"She [Gomer] doesn't realize it was I [The Lord] who gave her everything she has — the grain, the new wine, the olive oil; I even gave her silver and gold. But she gave all my gifts to Baal."

- Hosea 2:8 NLT

Hide-and-Seek

September 2011

I went away for college...

**breathes*

I can leave that mess behind me.
And we can too in this next story...

I was a freshman at the University of Michigan. A small cyst developed on the left side of my neck, growing massively. I was embarrassed to show my face in classes - *thank goodness for hoodies.*

I checked into Urgent Care on campus, and they referred me to the hospital.

The hospital??? My heart dropped to the ground.

My roommate and mentor escorted me to the Michigan hospital for admission. I was scared; I was 17 years young, without family in the State of Michigan, and didn't envision hospital visits being part of my freshman-year experience.

Tick. Tock.

Waited patiently for an ENT specialist to review my CAT scan results.

The results returned. It wasn't cancerous, but it was abnormal and required surgery.

I was relieved when my parents arrived during the first round of surgeries in September and stayed throughout my post-recovery for 10 days. When they returned home to Chicago, my roommate and mentor provided them with daily updates.

Finally, I was released during the second week of October but fell behind in classes. When the semester ended, I failed one of my courses.

I greatly feared being dismissed or placed on academic probation.

Cries heavily.

Unfortunately, the cyst returned and was larger and harder at 7x7 cm. I remained a student and a hospital patient throughout the following spring quarter. Luckily, the hospital cafeteria food was AMAZING! I had the best food and desserts.

By March 2012, I was tired.
Tired of hiding from people.
Tired of explaining my medical condition.
Tired of fighting alone without my parents.
Tired of walking through the hospital doors monthly.
Tired of pushing back academic plans to care for my health.
I was tired.

Tap. Tap.

Waited patiently again for these CAT scan results. This time, my parents were with me. The physician stated that they would have to import medications from another country because the cyst was too strong.

This surgery was riskier. The right side of my artery would clog near my heart if we proceeded. Death was a possible outcome.

Tuh! Death didn't scare me anymore.

I cried ferociously.

The medical doctor gave us space to discuss our limited options, and I screamed.

I wanted this nightmare and lifestyle to end.

Was the Lord punishing me for not obeying commands?

I thought I had been forgiven once I repented.

Was the Lord angry with me?

What did I do now?

What didn't I do?

WHAT IS GOING ON LORD???!! ANSWER ME!

"My God, my God, why have you abandoned me? Why are you so far away when I groan for help? Every day I call to you, my God, but you do not answer. Every night I lift my voice, but I find no relief."
- Psalm 22:1-2 (NLT)

I didn't believe the Lord was with me. No longer did I believe in Emmanuel.

I couldn't believe the Lord sent me to Michigan to die.

I was so angry with the Lord. I had no words.

I proceeded with my fourth round of surgeries to remove this cyst and missed more weeks of classes. Then, finally, in April 2012, all the cyst tissue was removed, and it left me with a scar on the left side of my neck.

While the nurses pat-washed and dried my wound, my physician explained he was glad I was admitted to the Michigan hospital.

Huh??

The physician explained that this specialty of medicine was only located in 3 states - California, Massachusetts, and Michigan. Had I chosen my top school in Missouri or North Carolina, I would have had more complications since this medical specialty wasn't available.

I cried uncontrollably. As the nurses cared for my wound, it felt like an angel telling me, *"I had you in mind this entire time. I never left you!"*

"Behold, I have engraved you on the palms of my hands."
- Isaiah 49:16a (ESV)

The scar on my neck is a sacred reminder that the Lord had me in mind before I moved to Michigan. For a while, I thought the Lord was hiding from me. But ultimately, the Lord initiated a search so I could find and be secured in Him during my most vulnerable time.

How faithful is our Lord!

Robbery

November 2013

...Time to return to more mess...

I returned home to Chicago for Thanksgiving break.

Waiting anxiously on my bed. *"Why isn't he answering?" "Are we still celebrating?"*

He texted back - "Change of plans. We'll celebrate elsewhere."

"Where?"

He was a private man with status. We did not have many options.

I didn't want to go, but I didn't want to disappoint him either.

The Holy Spirit tugged on me harder to cancel tonight, but I wouldn't listen.

Reluctantly, I climbed into the passenger seat of his bronze SUV and grew more anxious.

Side smile - he gestured and asked, "Why so nervous?"

A short drive to his home. He lived down the street from me. *"Why are we here?"*

He opened the door. Everything was dark except for the TV.

Unfamiliar with his home, I sat on the couch watching Fixer Upper, and he nodded once, expectantly, "Come upstairs."

No dinner.
No wine.
No snacks.
Just guns on the dining table.

I walked upstairs. Saw a glass block shower on my left and his room straight ahead.

He sat on the bed. Asked to take off my jacket.

He laughed and smiled.

Three. Two. One.

No smiles. All tears. All force. All "NOs!" were ignored.

"Clean up! It's time to leave!"

I *could not believe what happened...*

Should've listened to my gut the first time.

Should've canceled.

Should've played sick when he changed plans.

Should've listened to the Lord's instructions to remain celibate.

WAS *played the entire time.*

Manipulated by his badge to gain access to my brokenness.

Lured by subtle talks and smiles.

Entrusted him when I called 911.

Distraught. How could I dial 911 now?

ROBBED *and should've asked more questions.*

He knew the plans. I didn't.

Underinformed

He took

My consent

My preferences

My timeline

My choice

He took it all!!!

Body Aches

January 2014

My ears ringing.

Bowling pins knocking down one by one.

Another man has taken my autonomy.

Strike! Strike! Strike!

Perfect Score!

Can't see anymore.

Discombobulated in my mind.

Soreness in my legs.

Weariness in my vagina.

My heart was weak.

I can't feel my body.

These men caused unstable, painful rhythms throughout my body.

Make them stop! Leave me alone!

Body Aches

I'm hurting from keeping their secrets, sneaking around, driving across cities and suburbs, playing like a girlfriend, being a playmate in hotels and homes, being manipulated, being a toy for their pleasures.

Self-destruction

I cried for help.
Wept for days.
Destroyed every mirror.
Deleted every phone number.
Burned my black book.
Ate tears.
I looked disgusted.

Who was Antoinette?

My first name means "praiseworthy" and "flourishing," but my actions did not reflect it.

For 6 years, I lied to everyone.

I became a master manipulator playing double and triple lives and could not tell the truth even if it stared at me.

My worship life weakened.

I was dying on the inside while attending church. I felt like a prisoner trapped inside of pain. *Can I? Should I?* Reach across the pew and say, *"I'm hurting. I'm angry. I don't feel like worshiping today." Will that be acceptable?* I didn't want to hear, "Just trust God." *Is that it? Who can help me until I can?*

Can I give my heart to the Lord?

"But you, O Lord my God, snatched me from the jaws of death! As my life was slipping away. I remembered the Lord." - Jonah 2:6-7 (NLT)

I remembered...when the Lord commanded me to honor my body as unto Him. I thought He was punishing me, taking privileges away, and ruining my life. But He was trying to *save* my life before

destruction took over.

The Lord wanted to

protect me.

save me.

help me.

keep me.

The Lord wanted *me.*

But I did not listen.

I chose free will.

And look where I am now.

Pulling on the hem of His garment to stop the bleeding.

Body Aches

"A person without self-control is like a city with broken-down walls."

- Proverbs 25:28 NLT

Dear Readers,

If that was hard to read, I understand. Take a moment to acknowledge any uncomfortable emotions you may feel. Breathe and continue when you are ready to receive. Pain speaks loudly, but faith has answers. Let's discover them together.

PART II
The Placement

Closed Doors

May 2015

.... Back to college....

"What do you mean, I'm going back home to Chicago, Lord? This doesn't make any sense!"

Many signals were shouting at me that my time at the University of Michigan had expired:

No international job offers. *Denied.*
Tried to ignite a potential connection. *Failed.*
Rough patches and transitions with friendships. *A Hot Mess.*

But I was relentless and wouldn't take no for an answer. I ignored the signals and kept applying and interviewing for jobs in Michigan. Still no offers. *Another door closed.*

I could not believe I was going back home. I dreaded packing up items to return to the south side of Chicago and answering the infamous post-graduation questions, "So you're coming back? What's next? You have jobs lined up?"

Nope.

I went back to my childhood bedroom and cried because I believed the Lord wanted to hurt me, disappoint me, and traumatize me by bringing me back to the same geographical space that hurt me. I just knew the Lord had forgotten about me...again.

I asked the Lord many questions, *"Lord, if you wanted me to come back to Chicago, I could've stayed here for the past 4 years instead. I didn't have to move out of state and then return to this nonsense. Lord, if you want to hurt me, just say so!"*

No answers.

I hated the entire summer in Chicago. The one place that gave me hope and joy was my summer internship with the Children's Defense Fund Freedom School historic reading program, but my 3rd year felt different:

I wasn't present,
emotionally available,
or leading our team well.
I withdrew.
I was off.

My director, one of my spiritual mamas, knew something was wrong. She would ask how I was feeling daily, but this time she pressed deeper. She asked, "Are you sure, or is that what you keep telling yourself?"

I sat back and cried. I told her the truth. I could not enjoy this season because of my anger and bitterness towards the Lord. I lost faith in the One who was supposed to give me hope and a future. After many closed doors, I lost hope in Him.

At that moment, I was vulnerable like never before.

I shared the truth with my team and knew that this was another closed door.

Once the summer ended, I had nothing left.

Empty hands.
Empty heart.
No plans.
Naked.
Lost.
This was my "L" season.

I continued to serve at church, and one of the pastor's spouses who worked in higher education asked if I had anything lined up.

Nope.

She made a few calls, and I had an interview with a high school to become an intern college and career specialist for freshman and sophomore students.

Finally! A door opened.

While I thrived in my position, I still felt sick, empty, and disappointed. All I kept thinking about was time being wasted and feeling lost while living here.

Lost dreams.
Lost desires.
Lost career goals.
Lost hope.

"Where are you, Lord? *I've been seeking you and you're not found! Stop playing Hide-n-Seek!"*

Wait! This space sounds familiar. The same God that hid His face during my surgeries is disappearing again. This belief must be true—the Lord is not found when needed the most.

"Forget God!" I'll remain distant, too.

The Common Denominator

December 2015

Out of retaliation, my body returned to the mud of scandalous behavior. This time I chose the environments: new older men, childhood friends, bar hopping, clubbing, dressing loosely, and flirting.

It all crashed and burned.

I realized then why the Lord brought me home: **to face my trauma.**

"For they hated knowledge and chose not to fear the Lord. They rejected my [wisdom] advice and paid no attention when I corrected them. Therefore, they must eat the bitter fruit of living their own way, choking on their own schemes. For simpletons turn away from me—to death. Fools are destroyed by their own complacency. But all who listen to me [wisdom] will live in peace, untroubled by fear of harm."

- Proverbs 1:29-33 (NLT)

I sat in a dark room silently and had to choose a direction in life - either embrace this loss season or continue in destruction. Closed doors were signals to surrender my life to the Lord.

I decided mentally to accept this loss.

"Alright, Lord, you have me to yourself. I have nothing left attached to me or in my hand! I have nothing left! Now What?!"

"But if we confess our sins to him, he is faithful and just to forgive us our sins and to cleanse us from all wickedness."
- 1 John 1:9 NLT

I took a journey through my mind, body, and heart:

I wrote down ***what*** caused me pain,

where I felt pain,

and ***who*** caused me pain.

I stared at the list and wrote my name at the bottom - the common denominator.

Once I noticed it was *me* who liked my sin, I could not blame every current mistake on past traumas.
Even though I left Chicago for 4 years to attend college, the mess did not leave me. I did not renew my mind.

I grabbed my list and met with my other spiritual mama. We discussed inward and outward bodily boundaries to love myself more:

Your feet: Pay attention to the surfaces that you are walking on. Are the surfaces rough? Smooth? Cracked? Peaceful? How much more would you allow your feet to walk upon certain paths of life?

Your eyes are gates: What are you absorbing? Examine your vision. What you see can affect your vision and walk.

Your hands: Do you know what your hands are doing? Are your hands building up or tearing down? Are your hands productive or passive? Are your hands accompanied with pride or humility?

Your stomach: Are you full or empty? Have you nourished yourself properly? Where are you receiving nourishment? Do you need to continue feeding from these places?

Your mouth: What have you been saying or concealing?

Touch your heart: What is it longing for? Your heart wants to breathe, but what's taking up space?

Feel your body: Are you light or heavy? What has control over your body? How much have you been sacrificing? Are you recognizable?

I turned down my plate and cried immensely.
I allowed my body to go anywhere and do anything.
I allowed too many hands and words to control my body and lost ownership of it.
My body was tired of concealing pain.

I vomited the truth...

"Mel, I've been raped."

She said, "I know, baby. I know"

"People who conceal their sins will not prosper, but if they confess and turn from them, they will receive mercy."

- Proverbs 28:13 NLT

Salvage the Leftovers

January 2016

It felt good to tell someone my deepest pain, but now I am empty and vulnerable.

I had a cracked voice, weak hands, and scared feet. What can God do with that?

I was in between not going back to the mud, but not quite who the Lord called me to be.

What is this space?

Vulnerability.

A sacred and scared act that spells the same and coexists simultaneously.

Read it again.

How should I carry this emptiness filled with vulnerability?

Sit with it.

I looked at my emptiness to start over with the Lord. I could not do any more damage, so I might as well turn myself over to the One who created me.

But I did not trust Him immediately. Curse words, harsh statements, and silent treatments filled our prayer time. But the Lord was still with me.

"I see why the Israelites wanted to return to slavery because it felt better living in pain than living without it."

I took it one day at a time with change, but this emptiness felt like crap:

I left my baggage behind me.
Admitted my mistakes.
Repented.
Called and apologized to people.

Apologized to myself daily.
The adversary, Satan, offered isolation and pride. I fought back by staying close to my spiritual mamas and papa and kept saying, "God is with me".

But those changes weren't enough.

I still felt broken.

"After everyone was full, Jesus told his disciples,
'Now gather the leftovers, so that nothing is wasted."
So, they picked up the pieces and filled twelve baskets with scraps left by the people who had eaten from the five barley loaves."
- John 6:12-13 (NLT)

"Leftovers?" "Jesus cares about leftovers?" "Nothing is wasted?"

I was eating from bitterness, anger, questions, brokenness, and emptiness.

What can Jesus do with that?

And that's when I heard the Lord in March 2016,
"You cannot heal in the same place that you have been hurt."

I responded with a confused look,
"Where are we going with my leftovers? Where are you placing me now?"

Sink or Swim

July 2016

A new foundation was required.
It was time to learn who Antoinette was outside of pain, trauma, and trouble.

July 7, 2016, was the day I left Chicago on a flight with four bags and a conviction. This was the first time in my faith in Jesus that I stood ten toes down. I did not allow people to sway my decision. I no longer doubted or minimized the Lord's voice like before. It felt empowering to lead with my voice, my choice, my autonomy.

It was my Freedom Day. Not just geographically, but for my voice. It needed permission to speak a new sound - a sound of freedom.

Access granted.

I envisioned this new chapter to look favorably since I trusted the Lord, but quickly learned my ways and thoughts are not His. As I applied for jobs and gained interviews, He directed me to a temp agency placed on a university campus in Pittsburgh.

Temp work? Who?? Me???

I had a bachelor's degree from Michigan. And full of pride.

After a month of temp work, God led me to apply for a Guest Services Agent position at a prominent hotel.

A hotel?? Who??? Me??? It can't get any worse than this.

I reluctantly applied, and they hired me on the spot to learn servanthood:

Apologized to guests when I didn't feel like it or didn't believe I was wrong.

Took blame, cleaned up messes, and corrected mistakes that other departments made.

Served countless hours and probably saw the sun and moon switch positions.

And the Lord still wanted me to attend worship service and stay connected with my local church.

I was exhausted and upset that the Lord brought me from Chicago to Pittsburgh to a temp job and now a hotel job, and there were thousands of hotels in Chicago. *Like Seriously? Are closed doors happening again?*

Every emotion arose
Embarrassed.
Humiliated.
Played.
Like God, you out here playing me like a flute.

I wanted to escape it all! Because of my crazy and unpredictable work schedule, I couldn't hop on a plane and leave.

Retaliation crossed my mind to return to familiar muds. But I decided to do something different in this new environment, even though I saw no fruit from it: **remain obedient.**

During a particular worship service, my pastor asked us to choose either the desires of our sinful nature or the fruits of the Holy Spirit.

I wept.

It was the Lord calling me forward to either swim in the unknown under His restorative hands or sink further into my destruction.

I answered the call to work with my problem-solver, Jesus Christ.

Pittsburgh became a construction zone for restoration.

"My child, don't reject the LORD's discipline, and don't be upset when he corrects you."

- Proverbs 3:11 (NLT)

Dear Readers,

Environments provide us with different purposes to breathe, preserve, remain, develop, and learn. We may not know why the Lord places us in certain environments, but no environment is a waste. The environments we're placed in, will provide us with the nutrients we need to sustain the journey at the Lord's command.

Be curious about where you are.

PART III
The Plan

-- *Construction Zone* --

You are entering my identity being under construction
- my mind, beliefs, thoughts, speech, body, and faith -
from 2016 to 2018, and it can get quite messy.
Proceed with intent.

Jesus replied, "'You must love the Lord your God with all your heart, all your soul, and all your mind. This is the first and greatest commandment.'"

- Matthew 22:37-38 (NLT)

Soil

I was not alone while swimming towards transformation. The Lord sent trusted people to cover me while under construction:

My spiritual papa has been covering me since 2015. Even when I kept running to my mud and would not accept the truth, he continued to disciple me with patience and compassion and did not water down the standards of Holy Scriptures.

My move to Pittsburgh prompted many conversations about using this new location as a fresh start.

He said, "Toni, baby, I can sow the word of God, encouragement, wisdom, and correction, but if your heart is not right, it will swallow up all that goodness."

Soil
Soil can represent our beliefs placed in our hearts.

“The seed that fell among **thorns** stands for those who hear, but as they go on their way, they are choked by life’s worries, riches, and pleasures, and they do not mature. But the seed on **good soil** stands for those with a noble and good heart, who hear the word, retain it, and by persevering produce a crop.”

- Luke 8:14-15 (NIV)

He insisted I **change my soil.**

Change

I had primary issues with trusting the Lord and men, and wrote some thoughts:

- What do I believe about the Lord?
- What do I believe about men?

The Lord invited me every morning and night for solitude and journaling, and I could not resist His persistence. When I stopped fighting to be nice, politically correct, and churchy with my words, I saw how much we were flowing through every pen stroke, every tear, while every layer was being peeled off.

"I experienced the nakedness without shame like Adam and Eve in the Garden of Eden."

Assess & Unlearn

- The Lord invites you to run away with Him for solitude. Escape with the Lord to process your silence, anger, and questions.
- How do you want to process your pain? If you are a dancer, dance. If you are a painter, paint. I wrote through many journals and had many screaming sessions. Use your body and hands to process your pain.
- Habakkuk, Moses, David, Job, and others expressed their pain verbally to the Lord, and yet, we do not question their emotional intelligence or faith. Unlearn what the world and some churches have taught us to separate emotions from faith, but instead, integrate them with the Lord.

Allow the Lord to replace your soil.

Seeds

I had a messed-up soil:
I believed the Lord was a merciless dictator.
I believed men only wanted women sexually.

After digging and replacing my soil with truthful beliefs, I confidently asked the Lord to reveal His identity, as loving, merciful, forgiving, and other characteristics I needed to witness. I asked God to show me men who did not have a sexual agenda towards me but saw me as belonging to Jesus Christ. However, that required my participation to feel and **believe** in my prayers and **to be willing** to see something different.

Through this petition, I asked the Lord to **change my seeds.**

Seeds
Seeds can represent thoughts, images, and ideas that shape our beliefs and our decision-making.

So, I took my prayers seriously and showed up to work differently:

Served God's people at the hotel with the highest priority and excellence, even when I did not feel like it.

Prayed for guests and colleagues and had conversations about our faith in Jesus.

Met men who honored their bodies unto God by refraining from sex.

Established men as mentors who loved and respected me and my boyfriend.

This was the first time I felt covered, protected, loved, and nurtured by many people.

Ask for new seeds and new gardeners

Eventually, weights were falling off. Pessimistic walls, crumbling down. My trust in the Lord, kept increasing. I saw His character lived out boldly among people.

My prayers were answered, but this was not an easy or overnight process to change my mind about the Lord.

There were many days and nights when I told God,
"It's your fault!"
"It's your fault that I am this way!"
"It's your fault that you did not protect me!"
"It's your fault that you did not give me a different family!"

But, again, the Lord never left me.

I fought and worked my faith daily to see my prayers get answered.

Fighting **with** God IS wrestling with hope while enduring pain and disappointment.

Fighting **with** God IS showing effort in believing something different, while the present shows the complete opposite.

Fighting **with** God IS your faith response.

Remember to continue communicating with the Lord. Ask for new seeds and for new gardeners to sow and nurture those seeds.

"The Lord directs the steps of the godly. He delights in every detail of their lives."

- Psalm 37:23 (NLT)

Submerge: Uncover the Wounds

Cement masons and concrete finishers pour, smooth, and finish concrete for construction projects. While you are building a different foundation for yourself, you will need qualified, highly skilled cement masons and concrete finishers to provide you with the tools to rebuild your identity. My spiritual parents and mentors covered me, but I needed specialized hands to care for certain wounds with gentleness and instruction:

Mental Health Therapy

While I was engaged to my fiancé, my pastor in Pittsburgh started conversations about sex, sexuality, and intimacy during premarital counseling sessions.

My voice choked, *"I thought I had healed this area. I forgave myself already. Why am I silent about this topic?"*

A wound was discovered.

Wounds may not appear until contact is made, and my pastor found one.

When my husband and I moved to Little Rock, Arkansas after our wedding, I searched for a mental health therapist. She finished those conversations regarding sex and intimacy by walking me through her Psychology expertise and the truth of the Holy Bible. I also read many books, but my favorite to read repeatedly was Intimate Issues by Linda Dillow and Lorraine Pintus.

But something still was not right.

Physical Therapy

I was puzzled by my lack of sexual enjoyment during our first year of marriage. We honored the Lord with our bodies by abstaining until marriage, so why wasn't I experiencing the freedom and enjoyment of sex that God designed?

The Holy Spirit nudged me to discuss my sexual past with my OB/GYN. She was able to properly examine my pelvic floor and discovered much pain from the muscles that resulted from the rape. She referred me to a Physical Therapist for pelvic floor training to retrain my muscles from pain to relaxation.

My voice swallowed tears, *"The rape has ruined my sex life. But not anymore."*

Another wound.

After many months between mental health and physical therapy appointments, both therapists noted how dedicated and determined I was to become whole again. They've evaluated that I've mastered their exercises and accumulated enough weight to stand on my own. Like concrete, I would harden and gain strength over time.

Submerging is an action that will require you to take **ownership** of your healing to seek further transformation.

Submerge - *to go below or make something go below the surface [of the sea or river or lake] or to cover and hide something completely* (Cambridge University Press)

Caution: Submerging to face wounds may feel like re-sinking and re-living the trauma again.

It feels the same, but it's not the same.

It was painful to face those treatments, but I didn't give up on *me*. My future and my present needed me to keep going.

The Holy Spirit didn't give up on me, either. The Holy Spirit didn't leave me while I repaired and rebuilt myself, and the Holy Spirit won't leave you either!

Remember, we are designed to walk on water with Jesus and not under water. The submerging season is temporary; it's a posture of submission and humility to remain under and to face the wounds with specialized care. Go underneath with the One who knitted every part of you since your mother's womb. You can feel healthier and whole from deep within again.

You can do different and difficult things with the help of the Holy Spirit!

"He lifted me out of the pit of despair, out of the mud and the mire. He set my feet on solid ground and steadied me as I walked along. He has given me a new song to sing, a hymn of praise to our God. Many will see what he has done and be amazed."

- Psalm 40:1-3 (NLT)

Dear Readers,

If this section was hard to read, take another pause. The Lord's plan to restore us can feel overwhelming, hard, and difficult, but the Lord desires to see you well.

PART IV

The Planting

-- *Quiet Please* --

It's time for Holy Scriptures to soothe our hearts.

Proceed with encouragement.

Sacred Senses

Earlier in the Common Denominator chapter, my spiritual mama gave practical questions to assess body boundaries. Although we are heavenly citizens, we should not ignore our bodies. We should walk by faith and not by sight, but our faith should **lead** our senses that the Lord has given us within these sacred bodies.

For many years, there was a gap between my faith and my body because of shame, regret, and secrets paralyzing me. To relearn and regain trust in my body again to move with the Holy Spirit, I prayed over my senses with the word of God:

Hearing

"Then Naomi **heard** in Moab that the Lord had blessed his people in Judah by giving them good crops again. So, Naomi and her daughter-in-law got ready to leave Moab to return to her homeland.... they took the road that would lead them back to Judah."

- Ruth 1:6-7 (NLT)

Faith *heard* the Lord first, and then Naomi's body followed her *ears* to move to another geographic territory.

Pray for the Lord to restore your ears to hear the Lord's signals, signs, and instructions for your body to walk by faith again.

Taste

"Taste and see that the Lord is good"
- Psalm 34:8 (NLT)

Pray for the Lord to help you change your appetite. I had a taste for sugar and manufactured pleasures that satisfied my immediate gratification for validation and affirmation momentarily. It left me sick and deficient.

Ask the Lord to help your tongue taste how good, sweet, and nourishing His love is. The Lord is the living fountain that never runs dry or needs substitutions.

Sight

"Your word is a lamp to guide my feet and a light for my path." - Psalm 119:105 (NLT)

His Word is shining in your life, especially in the dark. Change your eyes to see it and believe it! Pray for your eyes to see that the Lord is ordering your steps everywhere you go.

Smell

"Then the Lord said to Moses, "Collect choice spices - 12 ½ pounds of pure myrrh, 6 ¼ pounds of fragrant cinnamon, 6 ¼ pounds of fragrant calamus, and 12 ½ pounds of cassia....like a skilled incense maker, blend these ingredients to make a holy anointing oil.....Consecrate them [these specific places] to make them absolutely holy....It must never be used to anoint anyone else....It is holy, and you must treat it as holy. Anyone who makes a blend like it or anoints someone other than a priest will be cut off from the community."

- Exodus 30:22-33 (NLT)

Our Lord is Holy. The Lord instructed specific ingredients to be blended to make holy anointing oil. Holiness has a specific, consecrated, set-apart smell. Holiness is the standard. It cannot be mixed with anything else.

Why dilute holiness with the common smell of sin?

Touch

"It's only the fruit from the tree in the middle of the garden that we are not allowed to eat. God said, "'You must not eat it or even touch it; if you do, you will die.'"
- Genesis 3:3 (NLT)

Unfortunately, there were many doors, bodies, and places with my identity that *shouldn't be there.* But because of my curiosity and insatiable appetite, I had to touch, taste, and see. Resist the temptation to touch everything.

Pray to the Lord for strength to resist temptation and for guidance to use your hands and feet to bring down Heaven's power on Earth. Let your touches be led by the Holy Spirit and not your flesh.

Bonus: Your Instincts

"So, Joseph got up and returned to the land of Israel with Jesus and his mother. But when he learned that the new ruler of Judea was Herod's son Archelaus, he was **afraid** to go there. Then, after being warned in a dream, he left for the region of Galilee."

- Matthew 2:21-22 (NLT)

Joseph received instructions from the angel of the Lord to return to Israel, but he didn't have a good feeling about the new ruler. That warning in a dream **confirmed** his instincts. Do not downplay or cover up your instincts. But rather, ask yourself:

- Is this the Lord's character?
- Is this my past talking?
- Is this brokenness speaking?
- Have I encountered this pattern before? If so, what did I do?
- What was the outcome? What can I learn from it?

I remember years of self-condemnation because I should have trusted my instincts before the rape, and I did not believe the Lord protected me. After much mental health and physical therapy, I forgave myself because I did hear God's voice that night. I did feel the Lord nudging me to stay home. Even though I ignored my instincts, the Lord protected me during the attack. The Lord's warnings confirmed my instincts, just as the angel's warning in a dream confirmed Joseph's.

Forgive yourself for ignoring, covering up, or downplaying your instincts. Yes, you have made some unfortunate decisions, but next time, with the help of your community and therapists, you can trust yourself again to make different decisions using your sacred senses.

Trust and believe your body can move in sync with the Holy Spirit again.

Continue the Journey: Pour Again

*"Then Samuel went home to Ramah, and Saul returned to his house at Gibeah of Saul. Samuel never went to meet with Saul again, but **he mourned constantly** for him. And the Lord was sorry he had ever made Saul king of Israel."*

- 1 Samuel 15:34-35 (NLT)

Due to Saul's disobedience in 1 Samuel 15, the Lord rejected him as king, and Samuel separated from Saul. That separation, without closure, understanding, or resolution, hurt Samuel so deeply that he mourned constantly for their connection. He did not know how to move forward with his grief since separating from Saul. Can you relate?

You had a deep connection with someone, an organization, an assignment, a location, and suddenly it ended abruptly without explanation, warning, or even an exit plan. Perhaps an issue occurred that ended the connection, but there was no resolution or guidance on how to move forward without them.

"The Lord said to Samuel, 'How long will you mourn for Saul, since I have rejected him as king over Israel? You have mourned long enough for Saul. I have rejected him as king of Israel, ***so fill your flask*** *with olive oil and* ***go to Bethlehem.'"***

- 1 Samuel 16:1 (NLT)

Was God placing a time limit on Samuel's grief? Was God insensitive? It's a fair synopsis!

However, God provided Samuel instructions on how to move forward without Saul — **remember your calling.** Separation is a reminder that our anointing, the oil, our gifts, our skills belong to the Lord, and it is not assigned to one person, one church, one career, one organization, or one environment. Samuel poured oil once before when he anointed Saul in 1 Samuel 10:1, so he needed a reminder to do it again; because the oil and Samuel belonged to the Lord and not to Saul.

You can experience life again after separation

Pain presents a strong case that it’s impossible to move forward without them. Pain can even block us from seeing the totality of who the Lord is. But our Lord presents a stronger case that He is **THE** source of all things. All resources on Earth come from the Lord. The Lord has unlimited supply for us to pour and that’s hope for us!

Here's what I love about our Lord regarding grief and pain: He asked **how long**. He did not say **stop**. Samuel probably took his grief with him as he obeyed the Lord to anoint the next king. Take your pain, grief, and questions with you as you obey the Lord!

What if Samuel stopped along his journey? Picture this: Isaiah 9:6-7 and 11:1-2 prophesied that the Messiah would come through David's lineage, and this prophecy was fulfilled 42 generations later when Joseph, a descendant of David (Matt 1), married Mary. Without Samuel's obedience to keep moving through the journey, there would be no Jesse, no David, no Joseph, no Jesus. God had bigger plans beyond Samuel's grief! What a full-circle moment!

Lord, remind me of my life's calling. It's hard to see my purpose while living in pain

Ask the Lord to fill up your horns with oil to continue the journey with grief, disappointment, sadness, questions, anger, and without closure. I encourage you to continue the journey in your obedience and faithfulness to the Lord.

You can pour again because the Lord's supply is unlimited.

Dear Readers,

Pain hurts, but our Lord is stronger.
You can move forward and have an abundant life after
pain and separation.
You can pour again.

A Conclusion To This Side Of You Does Not Have To End

You are

Shedding,

Confessing,

Addressing

Your pain.

Mending the soft, innocent, precious sides of you that were bruised.

I'm proud of you for transforming.

Pain started, but Faith finished.

The Alpha and the Omega,

Doesn't stop in the middle or incompletes.

The Lord is with us,

Desiring we live and look like Him - whole, holy, full, abundant.

We can't do it while hiding pain and living broken.

The Problem-Solver walks with you.

The Faithful One loves you,

Wanting to continue writing your story.

How should we end this journey?

Does it have to end?

Trust the Lord with your pain
The Lord wants to restore you

*"And after you have suffered a little while, the God of all grace, who has called you to his eternal glory in Christ, will **himself** restore, confirm, strengthen, and establish **YOU!**"*

\- 1 Peter 5:10 (ESV)

Bonus Resource:

Scriptures to Remain in the Lord

It is hard to see God's promises while living in pain and undergoing the restorative process. Speak these scriptures to remain strong in the Lord:

God redeems after sin

Hosea 2:14-15 New Living Translation (NLT): "But then I [the Lord] will win her [Gomer] back once again. I will lead her into the desert and speak tenderly to her there. I will return her vineyards to her and transform the Valley of Trouble into a gateway of hope. She will give herself to me there, as she did long ago when she was young, when I freed her from her captivity in Egypt."

God delivers restoration after pain

Jeremiah 29:14 (NLT): "I will be found by you," says the Lord. "I will end your captivity and restore your fortunes. I will gather you out of the nations where I sent you and will bring you home again to your own land."

God forgives

1 John 1:9 (NLT): "But if we confess our sins to him, he is faithful and just to forgive us our sins and to cleanse us from all wickedness."

God delivers His presence wherever we go

Joshua 1:1-5 (NLT) summarizes: "'I [The Lord] promise you what I promised Moses: 'Wherever you set foot, you will be on land I have given you .... No one will be able to stand against you as long as you live. For I will be with you as I was with Moses. I [The Lord] will not fail you or abandon you.'"

God delivers strength and encouragement during transitions

Joshua 1:6 (NLT): "Be strong and courageous, for you [Joshua] are the one who will lead these people to possess all the land I [The Lord] swore to their ancestors I would give them."

God delivers a fresh start after pain

Ruth 1:6-7 (NLT): Then Naomi heard in Moab that the Lord had blessed his people in Judah by giving them good crops again. So, Naomi and her daughters-in-law got ready to leave Moab to return to her homeland. With her two daughters-in-law, she set out from the place where she had been living, and they took the road that would lead them back to Judah.

God delivers promises after punishment

Genesis 3:15 (NLT): "and I [the Lord] will cause hostility between you and the woman, and between your offspring and her offspring. He will strike your head, and you will strike his heel."

God delivers mercy after punishment

Genesis 4:13-15 (NLT): Cain replied to the Lord, "'My punishment is too great for me to bear! You have banished me from the land and from your presence, you have made me a homeless wanderer. Anyone who find me will kill me!'" The Lord replied, "No, for I will give a sevenfold punishment to anyone who kills you." Then the Lord put a mark on Cain to warn anyone who might try to kill him.

God releases guilt from our hearts

Psalm 32:5 (NLT): "Finally, I [David] confessed all my sins to you and stopped trying to hide my guilt. I said to myself, "'I will confess my rebellion to the Lord." And you forgave me! All my guilt is gone.

God delivers protection during tests and trials

Isaiah 43:1-2 (NLT): "Do not be afraid, for I [the Lord] have ransomed you. I have called you [Israel] by name; you are mine. When you go through deep waters, I will be with you. When you go through rivers of difficulty, you will not drown. When you go through the fire of oppression, you will not be burned up; the flames will not consume you."

God calls you by name and not by sin

Genesis 20:6-7 (NLT): God spoke to the king in a dream: "'Yes, I know that you are innocent. That's why I kept you from sinning against me, and why I did not let you touch her [Sarah]. Now return the woman to her husband [Abraham], and he will pray for you, for he is a prophet. Then you will live. But if you don't return her to him, you can be sure that you and all your people will die."

God does not accuse us of our sins

Psalm 103:8-10 (NLT): The Lord is compassionate and merciful, slow to get angry and filled with unfailing love. He will not constantly accuse us, nor remain angry forever. He does not punish us for all our sins; he does not deal harshly with us, as we deserve.

We can transform our minds

Romans 12:1-2 (NLT): "Therefore, I urge you, brothers and sisters, in view of God's mercy, to offer your bodies as a living sacrifice, holy and pleasing to God—this is your true and proper worship. Do not conform to the pattern of this world but be transformed by the renewing of your mind. Then you will be able to test and approve what God's will is—his good, pleasing and perfect will."

You belong to the Lord

Ezekiel 16:8 New International Version (NIV): "'Later I passed by, and when I looked at you and saw that you were old enough for love, I spread the corner of my garment over you and covered your naked body. I gave you my solemn oath and entered into a covenant with you, declared the Sovereign Lord, and you became mine."

God's love for us is intense

Song of Solomon 8:6, English Standard Version (ESV): "Set me as a seal upon your heart, as a seal upon your arm, for love is strong as death, jealousy is fierce as the grave. Its flashes are flashes of fire, the very flame of the Lord."

Author's Credits

Thank you to my family and wellness team:

My hubby, Allan

Spiritual Papa, Pastor B

Spiritual Mamas, Mel and Jazzy

Holistic Counseling and Consulting, LLC

Advanced Physical Therapy

Countless pastors and mentors who have sown seeds into my life to see me transform from pain to wholeness

Thank you to my parents for listening and navigating through the tough and triumphant times, especially during my construction phase

Author's Contact

For any questions or if you need a space to be curious and free to discuss how the Lord restores broken vessels, feel free to contact

Antoinette Irizarry-Graves at
utterancemediallc@gmail.com

www.ingramcontent.com/pod-product-compliance
Lightning Source LLC
LaVergne TN
LVHW020640100826
845148LV00012B/2263

* 9 7 9 8 2 1 8 7 8 4 1 3 3 *